Thursday Motiv

From Surviving to Thriving in Corporate America

By Andy Hefty

Foreword by Scott Westervelt

Thursday Motivation

Sun	Mon	Tue	Wed	Thu	Fri	Sat
		1	2	3	4	5
6	7	8	9	10	11	12
13	14	15	16	17	18	19
20	21	22	23	24	25	26
27	28	29	30			

Thursday Motivation:

From Surviving to
Thriving in Corporate America

I believe in you!

Foreword

Motivation: defined by Webster – a motivating force, stimulus, or influence: incentive, drive.

Motivation is the process that initiates, guides, and maintains goal-oriented behavior, according to some famous folks including Sigmund Freud and his close associates. It may be worth mentioning that while these well-known men can tell you what motivation is, but they do not tell you where it 'springs forth from.' I'm guessing that might be up to you, the individual.

The personal example of my life may be an ordinary example in trying to capture the motivational birth of an idea. Now, if you are asking me, I'm just a simple man with a little education and a lot of worldly experience. However, maybe I can paint you my picture of motivation in the paragraphs that follow here.

As a Marine Corps Drill Instructor, I could motivate a platoon of recruits to move mountains with a few Bends & Thrusts and pushups! I guess they were mostly motivated by fear. Later, in training those same recruits, they would work their butts off to perfect Close Order Drill. I guess their motivation had turned from fear to a desire to win a significant prize and the glory that went with it. The initial motivation seen here is a motivation that was put upon an individual without their consent. Nevertheless, it accomplished a goal. We then see a second motivation that is generated from within; in this case, motivation comes from within a group of individuals who had a common goal – to win!

My example is probably more closely associated with the average person – an individual who needs to find motivation to accomplish a desired goal.

After I retired from the Marine Corps, I went into small business – Demolition and Hauling – with a small side in Scrap Metals. It wasn't much. I started with a pickup truck and a will to become a successful businessman. Armed with intellect from two master's degrees in business and thirty-five years of active duty in the Corps, I knew how to "Do Business"! My motivation was personal. I had always received my "daily bread" from Uncle Sam. Now, Uncle Sam had little to do with my business or success. I had to make it purely on my own.

I would soon learn that my new venture in business had everything to do with Personal Motivation. No one was telling me to be in formation at 0730, or to fall in for Physical Training at 1000. Now My Personal Motivation was telling me to get that ad in the daily news, to answer every phone call before it went to the "record your message" box, and to schedule job requests, even if it meant working after supper past sunset. I eventually built a pretty good reputation. Word of mouth began to pay dividends. Business habits like being on time, being courteous, getting the job done, and doing more than expected also added to my business success.

It amazed me one day when I arrived to do a pretty labor-intensive job. When the lady answered the door, she asked "Yes? Can I help you?" I told her I was here for the job she asked me to do. In complete surprise she said "Oh! You're here!" I said of course I'm here. I said I'd be here at 0800. So yes, I'm here." She said (nowt get this), "Yes I know, please forgive me for being surprised, but you don't know how many people I have called that said they'd be here and never showed up!"

That's when I really began to get a picture of the American work force. The little guy, the customer, gets treated like they're not the important person in the job request. Big business runs roughshod over the customer. That motivated me. Customers **do** keep score. They know good businessmen when they see them. If you want to be highly recommended for another job, act like you want to work. Appreciate the customer having called you. Motivate yourself to answer the call of each customer that calls on you.

I found that motivating myself, personally, would benefit me personally in the end. The underlying principle of this personal motivation I speak of is important. I cannot say what motivates me will work for you. Again, I had my full-time retirement already. I did not need to be successful at this business. However, my venture was a personal challenge that meant a great deal to me. My personal motivation was to succeed in the development of a highly successful business. It was strictly a personal challenge. Your motivation might be to build personal wealth for the security of your family and future retirement. Personal motivation may lead you towards Politics, medical research, or some other high goal that helps humanity.

Whatever your motivation is, it starts with a simple idea of what you want to do or be and how you will get there. When you decide to embark on that path, it will require Personal Motivation. That motivation needs to grow into a roaring fire. And it needs to be sustained by something I call "Gumption." An energy that comes from within. An individual energy that is so strong that it will push you beyond being tired. A need that will not be thwarted when the way forward is strewn with boulders in the path at every turn. And the need to live by a creed "Never Give in. Never Quit!"

As a Marine, I lived by an ethos that I would never quit. Quitting was not in my vocabulary. Quitting meant death. Win! Now that was in my vocabulary. I was part of a business whose goals were to win our nation's wars. Winning was everything!

Like my ethos and vocabulary, Never Quitting and putting it all on the line to win is a very good recipe for any entrepreneur to lean on who is looking for successful Personal Motivation.

Scott Westervelt
LtCol, USMC Retired

Thursday Motivation

Sun	Mon	Tue	Wed	Thu	Fri	Sat
		1	2	3	4	5

Acknowledgements

Unless otherwise noted, all quotes have been found on BrainyQuote.com.

Most song lyrics are provided via searching Google or Wikipedia.

Scripture references are from the King James Version unless otherwise noted.

All references to Author James Clear are either from his book *Atomic Habits* or from his scheduled newsletters.

No company is mentioned in this book, and no single company (or group of companies) is implied to be the "guilty party."

Thursday Motivation

Sun	Mon	Tue	Wed	Thu	Fri	Sat
		1	2	3	4	5

Dedication and Thanks

This book is dedicated to so many people, that it is hard to list them all. But here goes.

Jesus Christ. No introduction needed. But without His strength, without His love, I'd be lost.

My wife, Mary, and our 12 children. Their support and encouragement have meant the world to me. Without Mary's prodding me to write down so many of my thoughts, I probably never would have done it. Thank you, Dear. LuvU!!!

SgtMaj Ronald E. Fetherson, USMC Retired. My Senior Drill Instructor molded and shaped me into who I am today. He was one of the greatest motivators on earth. I owe him a debt of gratitude. "Aye, Aye, SIR!"

Jim "Pack" Barta, LtCol, USMC Retired. JJ Barta was my first commanding officer in the fleet. He was a hard-charging, lead-by-example Marine, fighter pilot, and leader. Everyone who served under his command would have followed him to storm the very gates of hell if he'd have simply suggested we pay the devil a visit. He had a unique way of motivating his troops that could never be duplicated.

Thursday Motivation

Sun	Mon	Tue	Wed	Thu	Fri	Sat
		1	2	3	4	5

Introduction

Why Thursday?

Why not Monday to coincide with what the start of the week demands? Good question.

When I first started writing this book, it began as a series of posts at a company internal chat board during my life in Corporate America. There seemed to have been a drag on people trying to finish the week strongly. All too often, people were calling the fourth day of the workweek "Friday Eve." That stretched a mentality that if we just went through the motions for two more days, we could relax.

I wanted to break that away from people. So I started bringing up little ways each week to keep them from dragging into the end. After all, when finishing a race of any sort, racers don't slow down at the end. They pace themselves to finish quickly, sprinting at the end. Thursday is like that next-to-the-last lap. Let's "gear up," tighten the backpack, and quicken the pace. Here in this book is the you-can-do-it approach to the cheering crowd near the finish line.

While you will find in this book a great many motivational quotes from people who have done this for a living, I am merely trying to show you how it applies to the daily grind of today. I have no expertise but my own experience and insight.

This book is intended to be read as a once-a-week piece. I've broken it into sections that seem to fit a particular mindset. But since you've already paid for it, feel free to read it however you want.

Please note that most quotes contained in this book were found on https://brainyquote.com while others are provided direct links in the endnotes. There may be some that are uncredited because they are either too common to provide credit or were extremely simple to find (such as song lyrics) by a simple search of the Internet. Anything listed in this book in the "quote" style is fully

Thursday Motivation

Sun	Mon	Tue	Wed	Thu	Fri	Sat
		1	2	3	4	5

Your Own Self Image

Thursday Motivation

Sun	Mon	Tue	Wed	Thu	Fri	Sat
		1	2	3	4	5

Let's have a list of famous people, shall we?

- Karen Carpenter
- Emma Watson
- Marvin Gaye
- Jennifer Lopez
- Joan Rivers
- Dwayne "The Rock" Johnson
- Thomas Edison
- Albert Einstein

What do all these people have in common? They all had problems with their own "Man in the mirror." Some were able to overcome the problem. For others, the victory never materialized. This list is by no means exhaustive. But there is a common feature: we often hurt ourselves more than others could do to us.

While there are definitely times you need to give yourself the verbal "beating" you may deserve, there comes a time when you may have over-hurt yourself. And I have two words for you: **stop that!** Author James Clear has some solid advice that I want to carry a bit further:

> *"The most important conversation is the conversation you have with yourself each day."*

What does that mean to you? I can only motivate you so much – same with others. The rest is up to you. Rather than talking down on yourself (how many times have we said something like "I hate myself" or worse?), it would do a great deal better to say something that would uplift your spirits. Try "they keep asking me because I know the answers and they don't."

Frankly speaking, if I value you all as highly as I do, the least you could do is see it from a different angle.

Jack London said:

"You can't wait for inspiration. You have to go after it with a club."

This is an interesting point. While I believe that inspiration does come naturally most of the time, there is value to "making your own." Rather than looking in the mirror and seeing your limitations (and I'm guilty of this much more than I'd care to admit), tell the mirror to either inspire you or get out of the way.

When you walk up to opportunity's door, don't knock it... Kick that b*tch in, smile, and introduce yourself.

Dwayne "The Rock" Johnson

I won't get into all the struggles that The Rock had growing up. Look them up for yourself. Know this…he is a textbook example of overcoming struggles. There are going to be times when you'll have to do a little kicking down of doors. Don't be afraid of it. Once you've introduced yourself, you'll have everyone's attention.

Make it count.

Success is not what you have done compared to what others have done. Success is what you have done compared to what you were supposed to do.

Tony Evans

Thinking about what you can't control only wastes energy and creates its own enemy.

Michael Dorn as Worf

Several years ago, my kids got me this tiny book of quotes from *Start Trek The Next Generation*. You don't have to be a Star Trek fan to appreciate the wisdom. Quit borrowing trouble. You are only going to make things worse by worrying about things that may not happen in the first place.

Imagine having a baby handed to you. Not an infant and not a toddler, but one that's in between. And at the very moment you take the baby into your arms she rests her head on your shoulders. (I'm using a baby girl for this exercise.) I've had that happen to me a number of times. Even when the baby wasn't tired, she would simply lay her head down.

Why is that?

Having been around a while, I think I figured it out: **trust**. The baby trusted me. She said with her actions that she would put her full confidence in me that I wasn't going to hurt her, drop her, startle her, or in any way cause her to lose faith in me. It's an awesome responsibility – and comforting at the same time.

Your clients do that every single day. While there aren't any tender moments involved, whenever they ask for help or support, they are putting their trust in you that you will not steer them wrong. They trust that you will guide them (and their clients – and by extension the entire world) into a place of renewed confidence and prosperity. By extension, the world trusts you.

Awesome, isn't it?

*Whatever you want in life, other people are going
to want it too. Believe in yourself enough to
accept the idea that you have an equal right to it.*

Diane Sawyer

My wife has recently returned to the workforce, now that we are
nearly done raising our 12 children. Plus, she is in school to get her
LPN (Licensed Practical Nurse). When she applied for the school,
she had to take a test and was told that 2/3 of those who take it
failed. I told her to stop listening to that. She passed on the first
attempt (and I had no doubt). She's been passing her tests (and often
getting A's), even though there have been lingering doubts on her
part.

I told her that she needs to believe in herself as much as I believe in
her.

How often do we doubt ourselves but not others? Stop doing that!
NOW!

Life doesn't stop for anyone or anything…Nor should you and your dreams.

Gunnery Sergeant Charles Wolf, USMC Retired

Gunny Wolf is a friend of mine who is the creator of the motivational cartoon SemperToons. His primary target for motivation is Marines and their families. But his motivation can spread to everyone. The point here is for you to keep the "man in the mirror" from becoming your biggest obstacle.

I don't believe you have to be better than everybody else. I believe you have to be better than you ever thought you could be.

Golfing legend Ken Venturi

Now…Go prove the naysayers wrong.

There's always a bigger fish.

Liam Neeson as Jedi Master Qui-Gon Jinn, *Star Wars: The Phantom Menace*, 1999

Remember, there's always something cleverer than yourself.

Nicol Williamson as Merlin, *Excalibur*, 1981

People with a sense of humor tend to be less egocentric and more realistic in their view of the world and more humble in moments of success and less defeated in times of travail.

Bob Newhart

Lean on me
When you're not strong
And I'll be your friend
I'll help you carry on...
For it won't be long
Till I'm gonna need somebody to lean on"

Bill Withers

Humility is not humiliation. Being humble is not placing yourself into a pit of despair and loathing. It's a mentality of saying that while your accomplishments are strong, no one person should consider himself or herself any better than anyone else. Each of us has strengths and weaknesses. Together, we pull each other up.

Do your best.

Give it your all.

Enjoy every small victory, and not just the big ones.

Use your strength and unique abilities to bring others along.

But stay humble in the midst of it all.

A real friend is one who walks in when the rest of the world walks out.

Walter Winchell

Consistency

Thursday Motivation

Sun	Mon	Tue	Wed	Thu	Fri	Sat
		1	2	3	4	5

"In baseball, my theory is to strive for consistency, not to worry about the numbers. If you dwell on statistics you get shortsighted, if you aim for consistency, the numbers will be there at the end."

Hall of Fame Pitcher Tom Seaver

What does that tell me? While management looks at the "numbers" for a team's performance, every team member should strive for improvement and consistency. Get up every day. Grab your coffee/tea/cola/cocoa. Give it your level best as we run this marathon together. In other words, just do your job well, continually improving your day-to-day habits, and the numbers will speak for you.

I'm no runner. Even when I was in the Marines, I hated running just for the sake of running. If you put me on a flight line to scramble fighter jets, I'd be running as quickly as the rest, and I would have done it all day, loving every minute. But to run somewhere, just to run? No thanks!

What I **can** tell you about running is probably something you've heard before that bears repeating. Our work is a marathon (if only it was over in just a few hours so we could collect the prize and retire).

During a marathon, there are times when you are running in large packs, smaller groups, changing groups, and just plain alone. But you're still running.

During a marathon, you slow down to better pace yourself, speed up when you reach an easier part of the path, or sometimes start walking to catch your breath. But you're still running.

During a marathon, there are times when a little water to refresh will go a long way to help you through the tougher portions. But you're still running.

During a marathon, you'll run into "the wall." It will seem like you want to quit. But you've been told (or you've experienced) that "pushing through" whatever is blocking you will give you an added boost, propelling you to the finish. It's painful and discouraging. But you're still running.

During a marathon, there will be times you can't see the finish line. In fact, there may even be times that you can't see just a few paces ahead of you. But you're still running.

During a marathon, you will either need assistance or find yourself helping someone who is pained – or both. But you're still running.

Near the end, you will see the finish line, surrounded on both sides by people who have gone on before you, cheering your accomplishment as you push through that last mile. It isn't easy. But you're still running.

You reach the end! You made it! You did something the naysayers said was impossible. You get your medal, picture, shirt, and the satisfaction that a win brings to you. You say to yourself that it was hard (or even that you'll never do it again). Something compels you to go beyond that and strive for more – for bigger and better.

So you get running.

"Never retreat. Never explain. Get it done and let them howl."

Benjamin Jowett

I've said this to many people, but in a different way. What I've usually said is, "prove the naysayers wrong." There's great satisfaction when your work and your accomplishments do the bragging for you.

"For success, attitude is equally as important as ability."

Walter Scott

Let's talk baseball for a minute, shall we? When a team is playing well, a great deal of it has to do with what goes on in the dugout and the clubhouse as much as what happens on the field. If you have a superstar who becomes what is commonly referred to as a "clubhouse cancer," then the team will not succeed. Or even if they do succeed, they may not make it all the way to the top. That "one player" whose raw talent is overshadowed only by his ego can ruin the team dynamic so badly that the team falters – or fails.

And most of the time, it can be traced back to an attitude. Be sure to keep yourself in check. Don't be that one with the attitude that brings the entire team down, despite how "right" you may be.

Don't watch the clock; do what it does. Keep going.

Sam Levenson

Yes, there are days when 5:00 can't come soon enough. And sometimes, it's the quiet days that take the longest. If you are all caught up (yes, it can happen), and the day is dragging, then pull out that list of long-term goals and start working on something.

There were days in the Marine Corps when they would tell us to "do something – even if it's wrong." It's funny, but it has a deeper meaning. Idleness is an enemy. Keep moving. Keep striving. Try something new. Stretch.

A popular motivational poster has a picture of lions on an African savannah with the following caption:

> *Every morning in Africa, a gazelle wakes up. It knows it must run faster than the fastest lion or it will be killed. Every morning a lion wakes up. It knows it must outrun the slowest gazelle or it will starve to death. It doesn't matter whether you're a lion or gazelle. When the sun comes up, you'd better be running.*

But Business Insider[i] carries this clarification that doesn't take away the profound nature of the poster – it merely clears up a misunderstanding (emphasis added):

> *Lions spend most of the day lolling around and then occasionally sprint off to catch dinner. And it's not technically true for gazelles, either: They spend most of the day nibbling grass, and then occasionally bound away in brief moments of absolute panic. **But the point is well-taken: If you want to live out the day, you'd better be ready to run.***

Always Do Your Best. Your best is going to change from moment to moment; it will be different when you are healthy as opposed to sick. Under any circumstance, simply do your best, and you will avoid self-judgment, self-abuse and regret.

Don Miguel Ruiz

Now those are some powerful words. I want to reiterate something I've said many times over to those on my team. "All I expect of you is to do your best." And this quote hits the target. Let's go back to a sports analogy, shall we? In baseball, you have nine players on the field (and a designated hitter in the dugout for the American League). When each of those players are all doing their best **and** working as a team, do you know what that team turns into? Champions!

So…Champions! Let's grab your coffee, cola, or whatever you need to put on your desk. Crank up the music (try *Rise* by Herb Alpert). And let's win.

Tell the truth, work hard, and come to dinner on time.

Gerald Ford

President Ford took office when it seemed that no one in the United States wanted his job. Washington DC was fraught with scandal. War had separated families, figuratively and literally. Inflation was hurting. Economies became unreliable. And everything seemed in turmoil. But he took that office nonetheless.

Politics aside, he took the proverbial bull by the horns. And no one can (or should) argue about telling the truth and working hard. But what do they have to do with coming to dinner on time?

Frankly, sitting down at the dinner table with the family – on time – shows you have set priorities for things other than "the office" (whatever that may be). Being consistent about showing up to the dinner table with your family will let them know that you will only step away from it when there is a crisis so big that you cannot avoid it.

My father was that way. He was a Naval officer. In his final tour of duty, he was busier than ever. And yet, he enjoyed the work. But…he was home on time for dinner like clockwork. His work would sometimes call. He would tell them he'll handle later, in the morning, or that he'd be right over. And whenever he left immediately, it was only because one of the planes in his squadron had crashed. Everything else was able to wait – at least until after dinner with the family.

We should all strive for that level of consistency.

Some quotes from Winston Churchill. He was brash, arrogant, and irritable. But at times, quite inspirational.

> *Success is not final, failure is not fatal: it is the courage to continue that counts.*

> *Attitude is a little thing that makes a big difference.*

> *If you're going through hell, keep going.*

I'll add this to the last quote: And while you're going, act like you own the place.

Vin Scully was more than a play-by-play announcer for the Los Angeles Dodgers. He was the last of his kind. He was able to broadcast the play-by play for the game for both radio and television – at the same time – by himself. No "color analyst," no spotters, no one else. He not only knew the game, but he knew the **people**. He would go to the visiting clubhouse to talk to the players, coaches, and staff. He would speak with the stadium workers. He knew all of baseball and could bring it to our ears in such a way that we knew all of baseball.

So, taking a cue from the late Mr. Scully, I'll "shut up."

That really is my trademark. Day to day, week in, week out. If something happens and the crowd roars, I shut up.

The game is just one long conversation, and I'm anticipating that, and I will say things like 'Did you know that?' or 'You're probably wondering why.' I'm really just conversing rather than just doing play-by-play. I never thought of myself as having a style. I don't use key words. And the best thing I do? I shut up.

As long as you live, keep smiling because it brightens everybody's day.

Don't let the winds blow your dreams away... or steal your faith in God.

One of my favorite expressions ever uttered by a player is Roy Campanella's line about how, in order to be a major-league player, you have to have a lot of little boy in you.

Be a bobbed cork: When you are pushed down, bob up.

In the 1994 movie *Star Trek: Generations*, you have this short dialog in the opening scene between two members of the original cast of the famed sci-fi franchise:

Kirk: Scotty, it absolutely amazes me.

Scotty: And what would that be, sir?

Kirk: [glancing at Demora at her station] Sulu. When did he find time for a family?

Scotty: Well, like you always say, if something's important, you make the time. Finding retirement a little lonely, are we?

Kirk: You know, I'm glad you're an engineer. With tact like that, you'd make a lousy psychiatrist.

While Scotty was certainly not the best person to break the news to Captain Kirk (or maybe he was), the reminder about **making** time for what's important serves as a strong reminder. How often do we tell people that we "don't have the time" for something? I even remember in a long-ago job where a fellow manager was told that he needed to take a time-management class. He told the executives that he didn't have time for it. That's **precisely** why they sent him.

The point of this page is to encourage you to do more than **take** the time for what's important in your life. **You need to make the time for it.** Set priorities. Set boundaries. Eventually that time will pass. Will it be a memory – or a regret?

Old vs. New

Thursday Motivation

Sun	Mon	Tue	Wed	Thu	Fri	Sat
		1	2	3	4	5

There's an axiom that "old keys don't open new doors." In the business world, that is more true today than ever before. The worst excuse provided by people who resist change is "we've always done it that way." Frankly, if that's the only reason to oppose something new, then the argument is weak.

By nature, I'm a man of tradition. There are times and circumstances when the "old ways" are the only ways. But there must be a balance. We must always consider whether the traditions of the past are a hindrance to progress. As we learn, grow, and adapt to the ever-changing world around us, we must keep an eye on the things that would slow down the progress.

The Saturn Car company was started as a "shadow-owned" organization that General Motors put together to try to revitalize the auto industry. At first, it was met with great success. The secret? Simple. They started out in a board room with a brand-new drawing board. It was symbolic of rejecting any/all of the traditional ways of yesterday's Detroit and making a new car company with no ties to the past.

After its success grew, GM made the most fatal mistake possible – they took over. They started requiring that Saturn comply with GM's "traditional ways." When the 2008/09 auto-industry bailout occurred, Saturn fell victim to the cutbacks that GM had to make because, by that time, Saturn was no longer distinguishable from any other division within GM. In a case like this, the old ways can be fatal to a company.

The lesson is simple: when trying to move forward, don't look back.

*I look to the future because that's where I'm going
to spend the rest of my life.*

George Burns

How many times do we find ourselves looking back to the "glory days" in our lives? While there truly are in some cases better times in the past, the responsibility to make the future brighter for ourselves and others is directly on us. The past is no longer an option. Let's make something of what lies ahead.

When Autumn strikes for those in the northern hemisphere, the leaves are turning all manner of beautiful colors. When I lived in Maryland, we would take the family to West Virginia to go see the trees along the famous Skyline Drive. Stunning. Out in the Midwest, farmers are harvesting. In places like Arizona, Florida, and southern California, the weather is a little less balmy. And everywhere you go, there's "pumpkin spice" everything. I even saw a car-repair shop sign saying they had pumpkin spice tires for sale.

In the southern hemisphere, it's Spring. New flowers, budding trees, pleasant weather. Of course, our friends in places like the Philippines, Singapore, Tunisia, and India mean they've gone from sweltering heat to … sweltering heat.

A change of seasons often reminds us that life and work are both chock full of change. Many don't like change. I'm as traditional as Tevye in *Fiddler on the Roof.* But if you don't embrace or at least recognize change, it will run you over. Look for ways to adapt. And in the midst of it, if you discover that something ahead is perilous, then it's up to you to "change the change."

In the dead of winter, we need a good reminder that winter has a purpose, not just in the earth but in our lives as well. Of course I can hear some people thinking, "You live in Florida; what do you know about winter?" Believe me, I spent many harsh winters over the years when I lived in places like Maryland, the mountains of New Mexico, Japan, and other areas.

What I appreciate about winter is what it does to the world. While many people see excessive darkness the "death" of their trees & grass, it's what's happening beneath the surface that should have you excited. First of all, when's the last time you saw a mosquito in Wisconsin? But beyond that (and I'm no expert), the ground is renewing itself. The snow seeps into the soil, not only refreshing the soil, but washing away toxins, making ready for a beautifully blooming spring. When the dead leaves and bark have all been cleared out, and there's nothing but the barrenness of twig & branch along with the crunch of dry grass, deep in the roots lie the growth of another year.

The same holds true for our own lives – and I am reminding myself of this as I type. Don't worry about what's on the surface when things go "brown & ugly." Work on the roots, the soil, and the underpinnings of your life and career. So that when a new season in your life arrives, you'll see even more growth and beauty than you ever thought possible.

Blink

And just like that, a new year starts!

Optimist: Glass half full: "New year, new me, and look at all that beautiful snow!"

Pessimist: Glass half empty: "Great, another 2020."

Realist: Glass half: "Busy season, folks. Let's get to it."

Opportunist: Puts two ice cubes and a shot of whiskey into the glass, raises it up, and says: "The year is mine to conquer!"

I'm sure there's at least a little bit of these in everyone. And yes, it's hard sometime to keep the pessimist at bay while preventing the optimist from driving you nuts with the smiles and attitude. Let's strive to see how much of the opportunist in us will rise up and conquer the day, month, season, and year.

Don't let yesterday use up too much of today.

*Even if you're on the right track, you'll get run
over if you just sit there.*

Will Rogers

He was a funny man, but his comedy held so much truth, that it's
now timeless. Put bluntly, don't look back for too long a time, and
keep moving forward.

Bonus quote:

*Everything is changing. People are taking their
comedians seriously and the politicians as a joke.*

*The good old days weren't always good, and
tomorrow ain't as bad as it seems.*

Billy Joel, 1983

Looking back can be a good thing. There are advantages to seeing
where you've been so you can measure your success up until this
point. Milestones are a solid reference point. And as Ronald
Reagan pointed out, it doesn't hurt to "close my eyes for an
occasional rerun" in life. But the past is indeed behind us. And
we're not going in that direction. The future is yours to not only
look forward to, but to shape and mold – today. You want a bright
future? Good. So do I. Let's work together to make it bright for
ourselves and those who follow us.

Leave Yesterday Behind.

Dr. Tony Evans

Milestones are great to have in your life. In fact, they are nice to use as a way of measuring your progress or even closing your eyes for a pleasant "Remember when...?"

But we need to remember that using the past as a crutch will hinder us from moving forward for the future. Past accomplishments give us the path toward greater accomplishments. One of my old Commanding Officers told me when he promoted me to Sergeant: "I'm not promoting you based on what you've done, but what I expect of you in the future." Each of you has been placed where you are to position yourselves for great things to be done in the coming days, weeks, months, and years.

Let's make it work.

In the year 2000, my seventh child was born. Prior to this, my wife and I had five natural-born children and one adopted. We were loving the "large family" life. And while the adopted one has special needs (Down syndrome), we felt that we pretty much had things under control. Enter Gabriel. (Narrator: you know where this is going.)

Gabriel's first couple years started out ordinarily enough. But after he reached the age of three, my wife was noticing that he wasn't progressing as most children do. We finally had him tested, and it turned out he is severely autistic. While we never thought this was "the end of the world," we really were unprepared – at first. As time went by and Gabriel grew physically, he took on his particular "quirks" that many with autism do. He was obsessed with *Veggie Tales* and *Thomas the Tank Engine*. He had everything on their videos memorized.

As years passed, and he was learning in school as much as was possible, he also grew violent. (Narrator: this is where the hardship comes in.)

Those who grew up "old school" would sometimes chime in with things like "he just needs a good whooping." Well, I have news for you. The traditional ways don't always work with new circumstances. Not only was that not the answer, but it made things worse. So, not only did we have to change our "ways," but we also had to change our "thoughts" about how to deal with hardship. We learned to see things from a different set of eyes. (Narrator: here comes the lesson.)

For example, rather than assuming the screaming, flailing, crying child in the grocery store is merely not getting his or her way, we have learned to check to see if the parents are in need of some support – or even a kind glance.

We've learned that taking a struggling neighbor out for coffee or dinner is more valuable than "we should get together some time."

We've learned that calling a hurting or mourning or bed-ridden friend does more than "call me if you need me."

We've learned that having pizza and colas delivered to someone does wonders over "let me know if you need anything."

We've learned that mowing your neighbor's lawn when you've finished yours provides a great sense of relief to people who are struggling to find the time during their busy season.

In short, you'll find that the "little things" are actually enormous.

Mistakes

Thursday Motivation

Sun	Mon	Tue	Wed	Thu	Fri	Sat
		1	2	3	4	5

From author James Clear:

"Successes are revised mistakes."

As I was taking one of the kids on a driving lesson, she hit the parking pole at the gas station. No damage to anything physical. But she was pretty shaken up by it. The lesson was hard – but it will stick with her on the reality of parking in something other than an empty lot.

Making a mistake doesn't necessarily mean the end of the world. Most mistakes can be recovered. We're not talking about the accidental gun discharge that kills a dear friend or running a red light resulting in fatalities. But there are times that you just flat-out "mess up." The key here is to own up to what you did wrong, understand where the need is to improve or change, and then strive to never need to learn that lesson again.

Come on Profile, you can do it. Don't give the
[expletive] the satisfaction.

Those were the words of Gunnery Sergeant Tom Highway played by
Clint Eastwood in the movie Heartbreak Ridge[ii]. When that movie
came onto the silver screen, I was an active-duty Corporal (later
Sergeant). I had a "gunny" just like him: Tough, battle-tested, loyal,
and fierce who callously treated officers who didn't know any better.
But he stood by his troops, even when they messed up.

What Gunny Highway meant in his words to a young Marine who
made a serious safety violation was that you may have screwed up
badly, but it's not the end of the world. That fictional young Marine,
named Profile, picked himself up, shouted "RECON!" (the name of
their platoon), and motivated himself to get moving.

Some days feel like that, even for me. But we cannot let the bad
days get the best of us. Sometimes I will play the song *Bad Day* by
Daniel Powter. It didn't change the reality around me, but it did help
change the outlook.

Gunny Highway believed in his Marines. I believe in you.

Whatever it may be, don't give your [expletive] the satisfaction,
either. You can do it.

If you're not making mistakes, then you're not doing anything. I'm positive that a doer makes mistakes.

Championship basketball coach John Wooden

Take chances. Make mistakes. Get messy!

Liza Minelli, voicing "Miss Frizzle" from the PBS television show *Magic School Bus*

You might have guessed that I have children. When some of them were growing up, they looked forward to enjoying a fun, educational show. During the show, at some point the students would get discouraged. Miss Frizzle would remind them that learning requires more than just book knowledge.

Sometimes, taking a chance is the price you must pay to gain knowledge. Making a mistake is a learning experience – at least in what NOT to do. And getting messy means that as you clean up and re-organize, you improve the situation at the foundation.

Just like in life, the show has lessons for us all, but there are a few bumps along the way.

Why do you think she always opens the show with "Seatbelts, everyone!"?

It's interesting to see babies grow.

At first, they have to be picked up and carried everywhere. Then they learn how to roll over.

And scoot.

And crawl.

And stand.

And fall.

And toddle.

And fall.

And walk.

And fall.

And run.

And fall.

Before you know it, they're learning to drive and ready to "fly" the nest.

But unless the child is unable to walk due to a physical restraint, you don't see adults scooting around on their bellies. They're walking, running, driving, or even flying everywhere. Each time we learn a new method of transporting ourselves from one place to another, the less-efficient way is left behind.

Notice that "fall" is prominent. That will happen. But it shouldn't stop us from progress. Learn **why** you fell and how to **not** fall in the future.

In the same way, we build on our past accomplishments, but we don't dwell on them. Use the past for a foundation, not a destination. Keep forging ahead.

Impossible?

Thursday Motivation

Sun	Mon	Tue	Wed	Thu	Fri	Sat
		1	2	3	4	5

One of the most encouraging authors/speakers/ministers I've ever listened to is Chuck Swindoll.

"We are all faced with a series of great opportunities brilliantly disguised as impossible situations."

On September 6, 1995, legendary baseball Hall of Famer Cal Ripken Jr broke a record that no one thought could have ever been broken, when he played in his 2,131st consecutive game. Broadcasting that night for ESPN, Chris Berman said:

"Let it be said that No. 8, Cal Ripken Jr., has reached the unreachable star."[iii]

For more than 20 minutes after that quote, no one in the broadcast industry said a thing. The fans were doing all the "talking" at that point as they produced a record-setting 22-minute standing ovation. The consecutive-game streak was previously held by Yankee slugger Lou Gehrig, whose life was cut short by the terrifying, crippling disease, ALS.

Until that day, many in the sports world felt that it was impossible for the record to be broken, as too many other factors came into play (shorter careers, longer seasons, injuries, trades, free agency, etc.). But it **was** broken.

Sometimes, all it takes to overcome the seemingly impossible is an attitude that will overcome it. Even the Star Wars world reinforces that through process:

Rey: Is that even possible?
Han Solo: I never ask that question 'till after I've done it.[iv]

Too many people in our lives become naysayers. My advice to you is ignore them. Make it possible.

I grew up a Navy brat, and we moved all over the US every few years. When my family moved to the Philippines in the mid-70s, we hired the customary domestic help, one of which was a man who took care of all the landscaping, car-washing, etc., once a week. Manuel was strong and able – and willing to do anything for you. When we left the Philippines and moved back to the States, the task of mowing the lawn was left to me. We had a large lawn on the base housing. I was overwhelmed. The first time out, I needed a great deal of help. But then my Dad instructed me on something that has stuck with me to this day:

Break it down into sections.

I took a small section of the lawn, cut a perimeter, and worked on that section until it was done. Since the mower had a grass catcher, I would make the chunks just large enough to fill the grass catcher so when I finished the section, I could also empty the container. I learned to make it more efficient while making the task more manageable. And then I could see that it was easy to measure when I was getting closer to completion.

Andy, why are you telling us this?

Simple. The daily grind of work can be the same way. Look for ways to break things down into chunks with noticeable stopping points that make the task more efficient and give you milestones to see how far you've come and how much more you have to do. Clients and managers (and Sales) clamoring at you can be overwhelming. And there are days when you have to throw this method out the window. I get it. But whenever possible, try to break things down into chunks. The day may become just a little less daunting.

PS: I believe in you!

Your attitude is like a box of crayons that color
your world. Constantly color your picture gray,
and your picture will always be bleak. Try adding
some bright colors to the picture by including
humor, and your picture begins to lighten up.

Allen Klein

Just who is Allen Klein? For those of you a bit younger than me, he was the music manager who helped propel the Beatles to financial success.

Lieutenant General Lewis B. "Chesty" Puller was the most highly decorated US Marine in history. At the battle of the "Frozen" Chosin Reservoir, the First Marine Division was faced with insurmountable odds. Today, Chesty is the most revered Marine.

To his command, he radioed:

> *"We're surrounded. That simplifies the problem."*

To his troops:

> *"They're all around us. Those poor b@st@rds –*
> *they can't hide now."*

It was a real-world example on how the impossible can overwhelm us – if we let it. Chesty and his Marines picked up their gear, picked up their wounded, and picked up their fallen brethren. And they moved out. This seemingly impossible task was made possible by the right frame of mind in the leader and then filtered down to everyone else.

Earl Nightingale said:

> *"All you need is the plan, the roadmap, and the*
> *courage to press on to your destination."*

Put all excuses aside and remember this: YOU are capable.

You were born to win, but to be a winner, you must plan to win, prepare to win, and expect to win.

The Late Zig Ziglar

If Zig Ziglar believed you're capable, then I do too!

*...so don't tell me why we can't get them. Tell me
how we will.*

Julie Dolan, voicing a young Princess Leia Organa in *Star Wars
Rebels*[v]

I'm a big Star Wars fan. During this animated scene, the rebels are
facing insurmountable odds. Everyone is saying "it's impossible."
Clearly, the young princess disagreed. There are times when
leadership seems to ask the impossible of you. I'll give you my
point of view. It's not because they have some sadistic mindset to
drive everyone bonkers. But rather it's because your leaders believe
in you and know without any doubt that you can stretch beyond what
you've done in the past. That's called growth.

So, the next time you run up against that seemingly impossible task,
"tell me how we will" overcome and defeat it.

You can find motivation in so many songs. You just need to look a little deeper sometimes.

Why are there so many
Songs about rainbows
And what's on the other side
Rainbows are visions
But only illusions
And rainbows have nothing to hide
So we've been told and some Choose to believe it
But I know they're wrong wait and see
Someday we'll find it
The Rainbow Connection
The lovers, the dreamers and me

Jim Henson as Kermit the Frog, *The Rainbow Connection*, 1979

If you wake up and don't want to smile
If it takes just a little while
Open your eyes and look at the day
You'll see things in a different way
Don't stop thinking about tomorrow
Don't stop, it'll soon be here
It'll be better than before
Yesterday's gone, yesterday's gone

Lindsey Buckingham and Christine McVie of the group Fleetwook Mac, *Don't Stop (Thinking about Tomorrow)*, 1977

I once had an HR representative that had text scrolling across her monitor as a screen saver. It said, "Behold the turtle who cannot get anywhere unless…" So I looked at her and asked the question she expected, "Unless what?"

Her simple but profound answer became painfully obvious right after she said it: **"Unless he sticks his neck out."**

That has stuck with me ever since that day. **To put in the baseball analogy, "You cannot steal second base with your foot still on first."**

Success means taking risks. Sometimes it doesn't work. Other times it works. And that can be said of anything in life, not just in baseball and business. Think about Charlie Brown. He never got to talk to "the little red-haired girl" until he took the risk. How many times have you been advised by people to stay out of the limelight? I actually had a manager way back when advise that I avoid making waves so that I won't be on anyone's radar – just in case. I think that's lousy advice. Failing to take risks is a choice that (from my experience) will backfire.

Granted, you don't want to take unnecessary risks, but you can't wrap your body or career in bubble wrap and expect to race ahead of others.

Taking risks involves a lot:

- Creativity – you have to be able to think beyond the owner's manual
- Time – this is a precious commodity, so the balance here is to be careful with it
- Patience – one of the hardest virtues to learn
- Openness – listen to others at the same time, including the naysayers, just in case they have good advice

Above all, it requires a **willingness to learn from mistakes**, both your mistakes and those made by others. These are lifelong lessons.

*The Constitution only gives people the right to
pursue happiness. You have to catch it yourself.*

Benjamin Franklin

This applies also to your life, not just politics. And in the work environment, if you see a need to make things better (and you don't necessarily need to get permission), then get started. Take the initiative. Make it happen.

One of my Independence Day traditions is to watch the musical *1776*. If you've never seen it, you should. While part comedy, part musical, part Broadway production, the screenplay was written based off of the actual transcripts of the debates during that tumultuous season of America's birth. Of course, there are some inaccuracies (what is a Hollywood production without them?).

But near the end of the movie John Adams is distraught. He believes he may have lost his years-long effort to win all the colonies over. In a quasi-dream, he "converses" with his beloved Abigail. She reminds him of one simple word: Commitment. Later he finds himself in an empty Congressional chamber, singing and shouting the following:

> *For I have crossed the Rubicon, let the bridge be*
> *burned behind me, come what may, come what*
> *may! Commitment!*

Committing yourself means looking back only for the following three reasons:

1. To measure how far you've gone
2. To make course corrections going forward
3. To occasionally think back with fondness on days gone by

Commitment means moving ahead, surging ahead, ploughing ahead if you must. And it means to never turn back.

Milestones.

In the United States, our interstate highway system is marked every mile from one end to the other how far you are on a highway. For example, when I lived out in the countryside away from Jacksonville, my highway exit was #333, which was 333 miles away from the western border of Florida on Interstate 10. Rolling down the highway on a long trip, you'd be able to gauge how close you were to your destination or the state line – or measure how far you've already gone. It's fun to help kids pass the time and minimize their continuous "are we there yet" questions.

Wherever you are in "Corporate America," having measured points of a project or timeline will help you in gauging how much you've accomplished, how far you still have to go, and whether you need to adjust your pace.

As much as I tell people "Don't look back – we're not going that way," we should every once in a while look back to see how far we have come to at least see how much we've grown in our own lives. Then, once you've seen the bigger picture, you can forge on even farther.

Improvise. Adapt. Overcome.

Clint Eastwood, playing Gunnery Sergeant Tom Highway,
Heartbreak Ridge, 1987

These words became so prominent, that US Marines everywhere use it. Adversity hits us – from all around and often at the worst possible time. But what "Gunny" encourages us to do is look for new ways to get around an obstacle, be creative with alternatives, and strive to get beyond the problem.

The larger the obstacle, the greater the victory…and the stronger you become.

The Power Within

	Thursday Motivation					
Sun	Mon	Tue	Wed	Thu	Fri	Sat
		1	2	3	4	5

More from Author James Clear:

"Amazing social skills are a superpower.
The ability to deliver bad news in a good way is a
superpower.
The ability to de-escalate a tense situation into a
calm one is a superpower.
The ability to transform a lose/win situation into a
win/win situation is a superpower."

This is what you do every single day. You take a client's panic situation and help them get to a place where they're happy again. This is clearly a superpower. Too many times in a corporate environment, everyone passes the hot-potato client to someone else. That "let's get Mikey" person or department often ends up being the Support department. There are times when all the executives in the world, all the sales personnel, and all the engineers cannot do what a single front-line support technician can do: transform a client from angry to elated with a simple phone call.

Troubleshooting 101 and the process of elimination, put into the hands of the right people, will get more customers happy and ready to buy the next "shiny new feature" than all the empty promises a company can muster.

The Power Within

Thursday Motivation

Sun	Mon	Tue	Wed	Thu	Fri	Sat
		1	2	3	4	5

More from Author James Clear:

"Amazing social skills are a superpower.
The ability to deliver bad news in a good way is a
superpower.
The ability to de-escalate a tense situation into a
calm one is a superpower.
The ability to transform a lose/win situation into a
win/win situation is a superpower."

This is what you do every single day. You take a client's panic situation and help them get to a place where they're happy again. This is clearly a superpower. Too many times in a corporate environment, everyone passes the hot-potato client to someone else. That "let's get Mikey" person or department often ends up being the Support department. There are times when all the executives in the world, all the sales personnel, and all the engineers cannot do what a single front-line support technician can do: transform a client from angry to elated with a simple phone call.

Troubleshooting 101 and the process of elimination, put into the hands of the right people, will get more customers happy and ready to buy the next "shiny new feature" than all the empty promises a company can muster.

"My strength was never about the muscles they could see. It was the one they couldn't see, beating in my chest, that made me unstoppable."

Sherman Gillums, Jr., CWO2, USMC (Retired)

Gunner Gillums is a Facebook friend of mine. He joined the Marine Corps after I had been honorably discharged. He had been an accomplished drill instructor and was even promoted to Warrant Officer. Suddenly one day, he was in a car wreck that nearly took his life. It did, however, take the use of his legs and hands. But that doesn't stop him. He is now a nationally known speaker and advocate for veterans' affairs. He's been an advisor on veterans' issues to the current and previous presidents and is called upon numerous times by them. The media look to him for insight into issues surrounding veterans and the military in general.

So for you, I say this…let that muscle inside of you be the strength that gets you through, defines you, and makes you unstoppable.

*You can't expect to hit the jackpot if you don't put
a few nickels in the machine.*

Flip Wilson

Put more simply, you need to invest in your own greatness. Don't worry about the enormous talents of someone else. Work with what you have in your talent pool and grow it from there.

Set your goals high, and don't stop till you get there.

Bo Jackson

"Bo knows." While Bo Jackson hasn't made the same Hall of Fame numbers that many athletes have, his achievements are considerable.

- Heisman Trophy
- #1 overall pick in the NFL draft
- A .250 batting average in baseball with 141 homeruns
- 1993 American League comeback player of the year
- Yards per carry of 5.4 and yards per reception of 9.1 with 18 touchdowns
- Honorable charity work
- A Bachelor's degree in Family & Child Development

It's clear that Bo does more than "know" … he leads by example. So this motivating piece of advice is clearly worth following.

"I don't believe you have to be better than everybody else. I believe you have to be better than you ever thought you could be."

Ken Venturi

Right…? Don't look around to compare yourself. Just improve the one in the mirror, and you'll always get better. And I have to tell this to myself a lot of times, as I believe I'm my own biggest obstacle to success.

Well done is better than well said.

Benjamin Franklin

This goes back to the adage that "actions speak louder than words."
How many times have you sat in a meeting where there is that one
person who will drone on and on about everything that needs to be
done or why something can't be done? And yet, for all the talk,
nothing gets done. Think of that one person. Could that person be
you? Be honest with that answer. Pause a moment if you must.

When you are fully honest with yourself and have determined that
this person could in fact be yourself, then you can start to realize that
the best course of action is in fact … action. Rather than continually
talking about a solution, start solving. Let your work be more
powerful than your words.

Growing up, I listened religiously to Casey Kasem's *American Top 40*. Having satellite radio allows me to do that on weekends again. His tag line always spoke volumes to me.

Keep your feet on the ground and keep reaching
for the stars

What does that mean? It means to dream big while being realistic and aware of your particular situation. Don't let your dreams be stifled by reality. But you also live in the "here and now." Balance your dreams with your responsibilities. Grow. Learn. Endure.

There is no limit to what a man can do or where he can go if he does not mind who gets the credit.

Ronald Reagan

While politics may be polarizing at times, this timeless quote was on the 40th President's desk during his entire tenure in the Oval Office. He used it as a way to motivate his staff to just get the job done and stay focused. I encourage you to do the same. When it comes to credit, managers should be absolutely certain to ensure the right people are getting the praise that people deserve, especially if there is someone else trying to usurp it.

But in the grand scheme of things, people will know who the movers & shakers are and who are the ones who merely show up when it's time to hand out awards.

The world hasn't even seen my full potential. But it's about to.

Charles Wolf, Gunnery Sergeant, USMC Retired, Creator of SemperToons

"Gunny" Wolf is a friend of mine and a "motivation partner." While I use my talent in words, his are in his motivational cartoons. One day, he and I were chatting over messages, and he sent me this as we were encouraging each other.

Let this be your way of thinking.

It has been my observation that the happiest of people, the vibrant doers of the world, are almost always those who are using – who are putting into play, calling upon, depending upon – the greatest number of their God-given talents and capabilities.

John Glenn

I had the honor of meeting John Glenn in 1982 when I was stationed in Memphis, training for my new career in the Marine Corps. Of all the early astronauts, he was the most positive, most motivating, and most "down to earth" (pun intended). But his point about using your talents is vital to finding happiness hits home with me.

What's your talent that brings you the greatest joy?

During my time in the United States Marine Corps, I was an Aviation Ordnance technician, loading, launching, and maintaining the F-4 Phantom (Google it for awesome pix). Anyway, one of the pilots I served with wrote a fiction around the squadron we were in at the time – with the names changed to protect the guilty. An excerpt from the book (a conversation between a flight instructor and the protagonist – a young pilot who had just earned his wings) made me instantly think of how we need to tackle our lives.

"What do you think of the jet?"

"I don't know, sir…it seems like the big leagues."

Yeah, well, just remember this. That aircraft was designed to be flown by a Student Naval Aviator. You are a Student Naval Aviator. Now, you go out there and you fly that son of a [#####]."

…

Nate now had a device to reduce the awesome specter of this aircraft to a controllable entity. Whenever he approached his jet on the Flightline, he looked at it and said to himself, "Alright, you son of a [#####], prepare to be mastered."

And then he went out and mastered it.

You don't have to use any colorful military language in your particular situation – if you don't want to. But the concept applies to you as well. The situations you face were designed to be mastered by you, the expert. Even if you have to look at your in-box or your work tickets and speak to it, it's up to you to fly it. Now, you go out there and you master it.

It had long since come to my attention that people of accomplishment rarely sat back and let things happen to them. They went out and happened to things.

Elinor Smith

Success is a state of mind. If you want success, start thinking of yourself as a success.

Joyce Brothers

Now get out there and start "happening"!

While Elon Musk is undoubtedly a strange duck, he certainly knows how to innovate. No, I don't own a Tesla – yet. But what he says here is quite telling:

I think that's the single best piece of advice: constantly think about how you could be doing things better and questioning yourself.

From my point of view, one of the worst excuses for doing things the same way is "we've always done it that way." I won't bore you with story after story. Let me encourage you to make a story for yourself by questioning yourself and the ways you do things. Always strive for better.

First, some history.

When the first Star Wars movie (*Star Wars: A New Hope*) hit the silver screen in 1977, I was living in the Philippines. Dad was a Navy Commander, and we were stationed at Cubi Point from '76 to '78. Blockbuster American movies weren't released internationally like they are now. After we transferred back "stateside," one of my cousins took me to see the first one. Yes, it was still headlining for a full year after release. The family became instant fans. Fast forward to the summer of 1980. Dad retired, and we moved to Florida. One afternoon, he took us to see the second movie. As we walked out of the theater, he said with great authority (as he always did) and enthusiasm, "They just set themselves up for another TEN movies.

Turns out he was right. He loved Star Wars so much, its main theme was one of the songs that was played in the slideshow for his Memorial service when he passed away.

Now, to the lesson.

In the 1980 movie *Star Wars: The Empire Strikes Back*, Muppeteer Frank Oz playing the part of Jedi Master Yoda was unenthusiastically told by Luke Skywalker "OK, I'll give it a try." Can you blame him, though? He was being tasked with lifting a spaceship out of a swamp, for crying out loud! But Yoda rebuked him.

"No, no! Try NOT! Do. Or do not. There is no try."

When you put these words into practice, you can understand. If you merely "try" to do something, are you really giving it your best effort? "Trying" implies that you're not fully vested in accomplishing the task. To give it your all and to come up short is a far cry superior to simply "trying." Falling short is not failure. Giving up is. Not giving your best effort is.

Whenever my children say, "I will do my best" or "I did my best," that's all I ever expect. That's what you should also expect of yourself.

Start where you are. Use what you have. Do what you can.

Arthur Ashe

Ronald Reagan said two things that have stuck with me for my entire adult life:

There is no limit to the amount of good you can do if you don't care who gets the credit.

And...

Some People Wonder All Their Lives If They've Made A Difference, Marines Don't Have That Problem.

Having been a Marine, I'm especially partial to the second quote. But the first is quite telling. Don't sweat the accolades. If you do your job, do it to the best of your abilities, and walk away with a sense of pride and accomplishment, the accolades will eventually follow. It may take a lifetime before you actually get rewarded for a job well-done. But it will come. And even if it doesn't, you can hold your head high and proclaim that you had a hand in whatever success the rest of your company encounters. You may not see it -- but you ARE making a difference!

That was on the name plate of my Division Officer in one my squadrons when I was in the Marine Corps. I guess since he already knew his name, he figured that it was time for his Marines to come to him with solutions to a problem – not just a problem. When you think about it, that is the first rule of leadership. Don't just point out the problem. Bring a solution to the table. It may be rejected. It may be crazy (I like crazy ideas). It may be completely out of the ordinary. But if it works, or if it sparks thoughts in others to work toward a solution, then you might already be on your way to a fix. And you've begun leading.

The Apostle Paul said it differently: "Be instant in season and out of season." (2 Timothy 4:2 King James Version.) In this context, it means you need to always have a solution at the ready by thinking ahead.

Give me six hours to chop down a tree, and I will
spend the first four sharpening the axe.

Abraham Lincoln

A good plan will save a great deal of time and effort. And a good plan includes more than just the way you envision, but the ways in which things can (and sometimes do) go wrong and how you plan to work through the adversity.

So ... "Plan your Work and then Work your Plan!"

How many times have you been told that "it can't be done"? How many times has that cut into your soul? Why does that happen? Sometimes there are people (I'll call them "naysayers") who will say this because things didn't work for them. Or it might even be that these people just don't want you to succeed. But it hurts – deeply. It hurts because the underlying theme that people convey is "I don't believe in you."

Well, I do.

So, I offer this advice to you: Prove them wrong! Don't do it out of a sense of revenge. But do it to let those who said you can't realize that you indeed **can** – and rather spectacularly. Will you stumble? Probably. Is there a chance of failure? Sure. But the best way to get past the naysayers in your effort to prove them wrong is to stop listening to them. Don't let their noise, chatter, and droning get to you. Just shut off the loudspeakers.

Then…get with those who **do** believe in you. Get with those who will challenge you, perhaps even more than you believe you can do. Let a mentor stretch you, grow you. Remember that one of the most rich and delicious cooking oils doesn't get sold until the olives are squeezed. Gold is not refined without fire. Fragrance cannot come without the beautiful rose being crushed. The challenges will make you stronger and better. Sure, it's painful. But keep your eye on the horizon while still focusing on the "here and now."

I believe in you!

*A hero is an ordinary individual who finds the
strength to persevere and endure in spite of
overwhelming obstacles.*

Christopher Reeve

Always be a first-rate version of yourself instead of
a second-rate version of somebody else.

Judy Garland

You are the only version of yourself that is genuine. Everyone else is a cheap imitation. A forgery.

Most people give up just when they're about to
achieve success. They quit on the one yard line.
They give up at the last minute of the game one
foot from a winning touchdown.

H. Ross Perot

I also enjoyed the entertainment factor when he was running for President, when he said in an open debate, "Larry, we gonna talk about it or we gonna do somthin' about it?" These words have two short but profound lessons:

1. Don't give up.
2. Rather than talking about a problem, do something to fix it.

Make sure your worst enemy doesn't live between your ears. Self-doubt kills dreams. You are more capable than you think.

Kris Bryant

I sent this quote I found on Facebook to one of my kids a few years back. She was struggling with issues on whether she was "good enough" for the task ahead of her. How often do you feel this way? How often do you find yourself in a "conversation" of sorts, trying to fight off the downcast depression of whether you can "do it"? You find that your own mind is fighting you. Well, I have news for you. You **are** more capable than you think.

Back when I was teaching a Sunday School class to other men in my church, we were discussing ways to keep a marriage fresh. One of the men suggested "little notes." Every morning, he would make coffee for his wife and put a little note of encouragement on the cup. Sometimes he would hide the note in her lunch bag, attach it to her keys, put it in her car, or other easy-to-find places. It eventually became a game to them.

It got me to thinking. While I wouldn't suggest any of the romantic side of things with "little notes" in the Corporate World, how often do we pass an opportunity to send a quick word of thanks or encouragement to our colleagues? Even just an instant message? There are times when I would cringe at hearing the instant-message sound followed by "Hey Andy" on my screen. Perhaps we should consider changing peoples' outlook on those messages by once in a while sending an encouraging word to them instead of some "need."

Even if all you wanted to do was say that you were thinking of someone, it would mean a great deal more than pinging someone only when you need them.

Trust me…if I were on trial for this I would have to stand up and say, "Your Honor, I am guilty as charged."

Let's be a little better at it. Make a new habit. Send one "little note" of kindness to someone every day. And make it someone different each day.

I, not events, have the power to make me happy or unhappy today. I can choose which it shall be. Yesterday is dead, tomorrow hasn't arrived yet. I have just one day, today, and I'm going to be happy in it.

Groucho Marx

Question. What does the word "token" mean to you? Does it mean a "subway token" like in the song *Rhinestone Cowboy*? An arcade token from your childhood? Could it mean the "token Orioles fan" that lives outside of Baltimore (me)? Or does it have a deeper meaning, such as "token of appreciation"?

While at the Marine Corps League Convention, I received two such tokens in the form of challenge coins (I got a total of five during the week – but these are the more storied). I won't bore you with the legend of the challenge coin, except to point out that some coins are extremely hard to get. For those that give them away, they're often a miniscule thing to give away. But to those that receive them, they can be treasured.

The first such token was given to me by Johnny Baker, the Commandant of the League. He had very kind words for me when presenting me with a medal for my efforts behind the scenes for my work at the convention. He knew the hard work that was put forth by **all** the people that I worked with in my spare time, and he made sure that everyone was properly appreciated. So, when he also presented me with his coin, I was thrilled. Again, little thing for him, but huge for me.

That evening, I received a square "dog tag" looking coin that given to me by the Commandant of the Marine Corps, General David Berger. He was our guest of honor at the banquet. We were told earlier to **not** ask for a coin, as it would have been near impossible to bring 800+ coins for every member that was there. But after I presented the General with copies of my books and told him, "Yes there's even a poem about the gas chamber," he raised his eyebrows high, handed the books to his aide, and then motioned to her for a coin. To be handed this rare coin by the highest-ranking US Marine is truly an honor – but a small thing for him.

(sigh) … "Your point, Andy! What's the point?!"

Here's the main point: It may seem a small thing to you to give a word of thanks, praise, or encouragement to someone. That's fine.

But it can mean the world to the recipient. It can mean the difference between someone having a "terrible, horrible, no good, very bad day" and a ray of sunshine that is desperately needed. Be generous with the kindness. Overdose people with encouragement. "Infect" people with praise.

Struggles

Sun	Mon	Tue	Wed	Thu	Fri	Sat
		1	2	3	4	5

If you're ready to throw in the towel, I'm going to toss it back at you and tell you "Wipe your face – you're almost there!" The scene can be picked up right out of a movie. That final effort, that final push, that final blow will often make the difference in what you're struggling with all day, every day. As a manager, I've seen too many people quit "a foot shy of the goal line."

Consider what others are telling you before you give up. Pay special attention to those who see the bigger picture. If you have a trustworthy manager, s/he will be one of the better guides in that arena. Your manager can see where your struggles are against where the goal line is.

From a football analogy, the head coach on the sideline has the overall strategy. The offensive coordinator, in the booth, sees things from a different line of sight, high above the fray. So, it may seem strange that the play called from the booth differs from what the linesmen think ought to be run.

You've heard the old joke "The journey of a thousand miles begins with a broken fan belt and a leaky tire." While that's funny – and sometimes true – my retort is this:

How do you eat an elephant? One bite at a time.

What do I mean? Start small. Keep moving. Use "mile markers" to measure your progress. Pretty soon, you'll find yourself well past "I can't do it" and approaching "I did it! What's next?"! Some of the tasks that you have may seem insurmountable. But take a short, temporary look back to see where you started and how much closer you are to the goal. Not every step is progress. Sometimes, you'll run into setbacks. That's OK. Pick up. Dust off. Correct. Get moving again.

You've got this!

Let me share some baseball wisdom with you that bears repeating.

During the days Yogi Berra played, rookie pitchers would say, "don't worry, Yogi swings at anything." The veteran pitchers would then say, "yeah, but Yogi **hits** everything!"

Yogi Berra was more than just a good defensive catcher. He was also a solid bat, lost among other Yankee greats in his day (and it pains me to say it this way being an Orioles fan/Yankee hater). But he was batting alongside of legends such as DiMaggio, Ruth, Maris, Mantle, Bauer, and others.

His behind-the-plate chatter was legendary as well. But he backed it up with being a solid individual off the field and a top contributor on the field. But Yogi never demanded the spotlight or bellyache that he wasn't getting any respect. He just did his job, did it well, and let history be the judge.

Sadly, he was more known for his Yogi-isms than his play. Things like "90 percent of baseball is mental; the other half if physical." But people who competed against him ignored his talent at their own peril.

One other thing about Yogi…he's the only person in history to have ten – yes TEN – World Series Championship rings. No one else has that many.

Why am I saying all this? Because there should be a bit of Yogi in you.

- You show up and do your jobs well in the presence of a highly qualified set of teammates.
- You give anything a try – and you end up succeeding.
- Your efforts are solid – day by day in what seems to be a long-grinding season.
- You lead in "championship rings."
- Clients, competitors, and yes even some of our colleagues ignore you at their own peril.

(Continue to) Be like Yogi.

"If you're trying to achieve, there will be roadblocks. I've had them; everybody has had them. But obstacles don't have to stop you. If you run into a wall, don't turn around and give up. Figure out how to climb it, go through it, or work around it."

Michael Jordan

What more can be said?

An executive I once reported to had some sage advice about obstacles and difficulty. This piece of advice is in a previous book of mine, "...*Always A Marine: Practical advice from a veteran's experience, expertise, and errors.*" Her advice is used with permission.

- Do the job you've been asked to do, but don't **settle** for it.
- **Belong** to the group, but don't let them set your standard of performance.
- Find a problem and **invent** a solution.

Each of these points drive home separate suggestions that do well to help in your career. Mix them together, and you can overcome almost any struggle ahead of you, whether alone or with others.

Never settle for "good enough." Always set your personal standards of conduct and performance higher than the minimum. And take the initiative to figure out how to fix things.

"Problems are not stop signs, they are guidelines."

Robert H. Schuller

Realize that the things that get in our way became a chance to excel. A challenge.

"Life is 10% what happens to you and 90% how you react to it."

Charles R. Swindoll

Chuck Swindoll is one of the most practical radio ministers I've ever heard in all my life. Plus, he's a Marine Corps veteran (so bonus points for me).

I will confess to you that how I react to situations gets the best of me sometimes. I have to improve on this myself. Let this be part of your own self-improvement goals going forward. Don't let a "bad hand dealt to you" define the rest of your day.

Taking steps out of your comfort zone is pivotal for your own evolution and growth. You cannot become a bigger and better version of yourself unless you are willing to stretch beyond what you already know.[vi]

This is vital to growth. In fact, without stretching, you'll never grow. Think of it like this: When you are training for a marathon, you don't simply wake up one morning, put on your jogging suit, and run 26.2 miles on the first attempt. You have to go start running, and then you run more than what you're used to running. The next time, you go further. Each time you lace up, you determine to make the next mile. But each time, that run becomes more difficult.

Once you have reached a certain "peak," the "next mile" might be even harder. In fact, it may seem impossible. But until you "go that extra mile," making the physical, spiritual, or other sacrifices necessary, you won't achieve that goal.

Yes, it's painful, but you can – and must – take that approach if you are ever going to grow.

No one wants to do any of the following:

- Eat raw flour
- Drink vanilla extract
- Sit in a 350-degree oven

But in the right mix, along with butter, sugar, eggs, and chocolate chips (among other things), **and then** applying the right amount of heat at the right amount of time, we suddenly have cookies! And who doesn't like freshly baked cookies?

There are so many elements (ingredients) to what we do, and some of them aren't very pleasant. But when we all are working together, and under the right amount of "heat" applied, we suddenly have one of the greatest teams to help clients.

Late in the 2021 season, my Baltimore Orioles snapped a nineteen-game losing streak by beating the California Angels 10-6. Of course, they were the worst team in all of Major League Baseball at that time, but they're still **my** team. The place went nuts as the O's decided to break out the bats and knock a few homeruns late in the game. Should the fans be celebrating after NINETEEN straight losses? Some would think "who cares?" but not me. There are times when the "small victories" can make a big difference – in baseball, in business, in life.

That win seemed to propel the O's to finish out the season strong and prepare for their old winning ways the following year (2022 was a winning season). And the same can be said in many things.

Like that time an autistic child finally asks for a drink rather than just grunting.

Like that time your Excel formula works so you can analyze the data and report back to management.

Like that time you had enough points for a free breakfast at your favorite bagel place.

Like that time … well, you get the idea.

While I am not in any way advocating a Pollyanna point of view, it doesn't hurt to look for the small victories and build on them from there. Come to think of it, maybe **I am** suggesting we look at things the way Pollyanna did.

Remember it only takes a little spark to start a roaring fire – sometimes you just have to fuel it.

Do you want to know who you are? Don't ask.
Act! Action will delineate and define you.

Thomas Jefferson

All too often, my personal conversations turn to the fact that I served in the United States Marine Corps. I never served in combat – I only served during peacetime, but I was ready should the need arise while I was active duty. These days, I recognize that I have **talked about** my time in the Corps more than my actual time I served.

But what I did – what I became – defined me.

How many times have you heard someone referred to by their actions, whether good or bad? "He's the guy who spilled coffee on the CEO."

While that is an extreme example, you get the point. Do something. Be known as a doer.

In our personal and professional lives, we are constantly hit with one adversity after the other, most of which we have no control over. But the four things we have total control over is how we react, how we adapt, how we breathe, and how we take action.

Diamond Dallas Page

These "four things" are nowhere near easy on the "scale" of life-action. In fact, they can be a daily lifetime struggle. So, if you have a problem with one of these areas, you need to write this down on a card and put it in your mirror. Then, write it on a sticky note and put it on your monitor.

When you're halfway through the year, what comes to mind? In some cases, the famous song *Livin' On A Prayer* by Bon Jovi, 1986. Despite the fact that I prefer 70s music over everything else, I really like this song. Besides having a memorable tune, it tells a story. From Wikipedia:

> *"It deals with the way that two kids – Tommy and Gina – face life's struggles," noted Bon Jovi, "and how their love and ambitions get them through the hard times. It's working class and it's real… I wanted to incorporate the movie element, and tell a story about people I knew. So instead of doing what I did on 'Runaway', where the girl didn't have a name, I gave them names, which gave them an identity… Tommy and Gina aren't two specific people; they represent a lifestyle."[vii]*

We struggle through this thing called Life (not the Milton-Bradley game – that's easy). And when times get even more difficult, perhaps even overwhelming, we have to cling to what lies ahead: our hopes, our dreams, and each other. Everyone struggles. Everyone suffers. We all have the potential to overcome. During these times, look to those who struggled and overcame. Be ready to learn the lessons they endured so you, too, can get past the daily grind and come out on top.

What does it matter to ya?

When you've got a job to do,

You've got to do it well.

You gotta give the other fella
HEEEEEEEEEEEEEEEEEEEEEELLLLLLLLLLLL!"

Sir Paul McCartney and his late wife Linda, *Live and Let Die*, 1973

While it seems that there are times that you're getting force-fed someone else's garbage, what you need to do is focus on the job in front of you, do it well, and move forward. Let your work speak for itself and let others worry about the tasks in front of them.

You build on failure. You use it as a stepping stone. Close the door on the past. You don't try to forget the mistakes, but you don't dwell on it. You don't let it have any of your energy, or any of your time, or any of your space.

Johnny Cash

The late Johnny Cash was an authority on this. He didn't let his own adversity get in the way of eventual success. And while it's true that much of his adversity later in his life was self-inflicted, he overcame his own failures and saw a way out.

If no one is there to help you out of the mire, let me know. I'll help you.

All the adversity I've had in my life, all my
troubles and obstacles, have strengthened me...
You may not realize it when it happens, but a kick
in the teeth may be the best thing in the world for
you.

Walt Disney

I'm sure you're thinking that this quote should be met with a big "No thanks!" But how many people have you seen (including the one in the mirror) that are made stronger by adversity?

- Orange juice requires squeezing.
- Diamonds are formed under extreme heat and pressure.
- Beautifully shaped glass pieces are melted, blown, manipulated.
- Marines can only earn their title after going through the "Crucible."

The best teams are formed under the bonds of adversity. Time to emerge victoriously – together.

Comedy

Here's a special section devoted to comedy. Laughter can be medicinal in and of itself. A happy heart does a great deal of good for people, and sometimes all it takes is a joke. You don't have to laugh at other people's expense, either. There are plenty of "cat videos" to find if you want. But from time to time, it helps to simply bust out laughing.

Thursday Motivation

Sun	Mon	Tue	Wed	Thu	Fri	Sat
		1	2	3	4	5

Steven Wright is hilarious – or at least I find him to be! His deadpan/monotone style is so funny, I end up in tears and out of breath after watching his routines. If you've never heard of him, search his name on YouTube. So...to give you a little humor today, let's hear from the legend himself.

Whenever I think of the past, it brings back so many memories.

Everywhere is within walking distance if you have the time.

Last night I stayed up late playing poker with Tarot cards. I got a full house and four people died.

If at first you don't succeed, then skydiving definitely isn't for you.

Experience is something you don't get until just after you need it.

I busted a mirror and got seven years bad luck, but my lawyer thinks he can get me five.

I installed a skylight in my apartment... the people who live above me are furious!

Curiosity killed the cat, but for a while I was a suspect.

Someone asked me, if I were stranded on a desert island what book would I bring... 'How to Build a Boat.'

My doctor told me I shouldn't work out until I'm in better shape. I told him, 'All right; don't send me a bill until I pay you.'

I have an answering machine in my car. It says, I'm home now. But leave a message and I'll call when I'm out.

My neighbor has a circular driveway... he can't get out.

When I was 16... I worked in a pet store. And they fired me because... they had three snakes in there, and one day I braided them.

Having 12 children, I can especially attest to the last one in this list (thankfully, the youngest is a teen now, so I finally have the lid □). Enjoy!

Behind every great man is a woman rolling her eyes.

Jim Carrey

A day without sunshine is like, you know, night.

Steve Martin

Procrastination is the art of keeping up with yesterday.

Don Marquis

I am a marvelous housekeeper. Every time I leave a man I keep his house.

Zsa Zsa Gabor

Happiness is having a large, loving, caring, close-knit family in another city.

George Burns

There cannot be a crisis next week. My schedule is already full.

Henry Kissinger

I cook with wine, sometimes I even add it to the food.

W. C. Fields

Weather forecast for tonight: dark.

George Carlin

> *A two-year-old is kind of like having a blender, but*
> *you don't have a top for it.*

Jerry Seinfeld

Below are various jokes that I love to tell. Some are military jokes, some are "preacher" jokes, some are Dad jokes, and all are intended to just get you to smile, chuckle, laugh, or at least shake your head and wonder whether I finally lost it. No offense is intended, as I have been in ministry (and I'll always be a Marine), so it's more of a little self-deprecating humor than anything else.

How many Marines does it take to make popcorn? Five – one to hold the pan and four to shake the stove.

Three Marines walk into a bar. Their sergeant ducks under it.

(This one won me a $25 check from *Leatherneck Magazine's* caption contest. It had a pic of a Marine looking over the high sage grass): Murphy's Military Law #6: If your sergeant can see you, so can the enemy.

What does it say inside a preacher's white collar? Kills fleas for up to six months.

How did the preacher finally get the bats out of the bell tower? He baptized them, gave them tithing envelopes, and had them fill out a membership card.

What do you say to a two-headed monster? Hello, hello.

Why did the preacher cross the road? To get to the other tithe.

What does it mean when the preacher takes his watch off his wrist and puts it on the podium? Nothing. He ignores it and keeps talking anyway.

How do you know you're talking to a fighter pilot? He'll tell you.

*One of the things I learned the hard way was that
it doesn't pay to get discouraged. Keeping busy
and making optimism a way of life can restore
your faith in yourself.*

Lucille Ball

OK. This isn't comedy. But one of the "queens of comedy" said it. So it qualifies here. Funny people are often hard on themselves. It's a struggle to stay both funny and encouraged. Remember to encourage the encourager once in a while.

Self Care

Thursday Motivation

Sun	Mon	Tue	Wed	Thu	Fri	Sat
		1	2	3	4	5

When the holidays are upon you, consider a few things. At the end of October and running through the end of the year, the list of holidays can be quite extreme:

- Halloween
- Election Day
- Marine Corps Birthday (I'm a Marine veteran, so it's a holiday for me)
- Veteran's Day
- Diwali
- Thanksgiving Day
- Black Friday
- Cyber Monday
- Tech Tuesday/Giving Tuesday
- Hanukkah
- Christmas
- New Years

Who wouldn't stress out over **any** of them, let alone two months' worth all rolled together? With that in mind, consider the following ideas.

Take time for yourself. Not your significant other, not your kids, not your family – for YOU! A golf driving range, overpriced coffee, spa day, hunting or fishing, sleeping in, whatever gives you that opportunity to give yourself that therapy you need. Do something for yourself. It doesn't have to be expensive. But it should be an investment in yourself and your time.

Call a loved one. Video chat if possible. Make someone's day by just letting them know that you're thinking of them.

Check in on someone that may be hurting. The holidays can be painful for some, whether it conjures up painful memories, reminds of a lost relative, or is simply lonely for someone. Reach out and be there – even if it's just a simple text message.

Relax. The party doesn't have to be perfect. Memorable moments matter more than whether the cocktail napkins match the drapes and tablecloths.

Improvise. While making Thanksgiving dinner one year (starting really early in the morning with my son because we enjoy it so much), I left a 5-pound bag of cheddar on top of the freezer in the garage. When I finally discovered it, the bag was bad. So the homemade macaroni had to be improvised. Kids loved it anyway. And life was good.

All you need is a love. But a little chocolate now
and then doesn't hurt.

Charles Schultz[viii]

I'm not a big fan of candy, unless it is chocolate. My favorite has to do with peanut butter, but I won't mention the brand name – you can guess. There are going to be days in your life where you need to indulge your taste buds. And it's not because of any other reason than the satisfaction that something sweet will bring.

Did you overcome that last obstacle? Have some chocolate.

Did you pass a college test? Have some chocolate.

Did you get some good news? Have some chocolate.

Obviously, you should be careful about overdoing it. But making for that special occasion to have a good piece of chocolate will go a long way.

*What they call you is one thing. What you answer
to is something else.*

Poet Lucille Clifton[ix]

This is as profound as it gets. One of the things I've constantly
harped on, whether it's in motivating my children, my colleagues, or
my readers is to constantly prove the naysayers wrong. And if
someone tries to call you a failure, then the best answer to that is
your success. If someone calls you a loser, then get out there and
win.

One of the best things you can do to those who would bring you
down is to succeed in such magnificent proportions as to leave them
speechless.

Don't let the critics have the last word.

Here comes the sun (doo-de-doo-doo)

George Harrison, 1969

Sunshine on my shoulders makes me happy

John Denver, 1971

You are the sunshine of my life

Stevie Wonder, 1973

I'm walking on sunshine (whoa-oh-oh) – And don't it feel GOOD!

Katrina and the Waves, 1985

There's always a therapeutic attribute to sunlight. I'm no doctor, and I don't play one on TV. But getting outside and spending a little time in the sun can be a good thing. Of course, you have to protect your skin, eyes, and so forth. But with so many still working from home exclusively, we tend to stay cooped up indoors. Even if you go out during your lunch break (you're still taking those, right?), for 15 minutes to let the dog out or check the mail, it's still more than nothing.

So perhaps when you are planning your next vacation (you're still taking vacation, right?), you may want to plan a little "fun in the sun" for whatever you're going to do.

There's an old adage: "How do you eat an elephant? One bite at a time."

Now, please don't misunderstand me. I have no intention to advocate for harming such a majestic creature. It's the parallel to a daunting task that I want to draw your attention to today. You are overwhelmed. Clients are calling in. Some are yelling at you. Many are being unprofessional (and that's putting it mildly). The more work you do, the more tasks pile up.

I get it. We're right there with you. So how do you overcome it? One bite at a time.

Wherever you can, set priorities of what needs immediate attention, what can wait until later, and what needs to go to your "focus time." Then start knocking them out. Easier said than done, right? Well, yes. But begin making new habits that will help you set priorities. Be sure to stand and stretch once in a while so your body doesn't fight you back. Have a diversion at the end of the day. Take your vacations when you've scheduled them so you can think about "not work" items. Get regular rest. See your doctor regularly.

You've seen the "Wanna Getaway?" commercials from Southwest Airlines. They're hilarious. Like the referee about to start a football game at the coin-toss ceremony asking on the loudspeakers if anyone has change for a dollar. Or the employee clicking the "Pink Slip Virus" e-mail that immediately infects everyone's computer. And the waiter that pops a champagne cork right into the eye of the mobster.

There are times for us, however, that we really do want to get away from it all. And you should. Whenever feasible, make the time (notice I didn't say "take") to have a weekend away from your desk. For some, that means curling up into a lounge chair with a book. For others, it means jumping out of a perfectly good airplane in hopes that you put a parachute on your back instead of your rucksack. For another, it might be the ocean, the mountain, the woods, or the open road. Or even tailgating at a college football game.

Whatever it is, if you **need** to get away once in a while (and you do), then you must make the investment and time (and sometimes money) to do so. Come back refreshed. The work will be here when you get back. It'd be better to take a break than to let the work break you.

Way back when I lived in Albuquerque in the 70s, I broke a finger (don't ask how – it's embarrassing). When I had physical therapy after the splint was removed, my mother would take me to a local doughnut shop for a doughnut before taking me to school. Now who can argue with that? It was refreshing to have a little treat as a relief from the pain. In the spirit of taking care of yourself, don't forget to establish and maintain some habits. Some suggestions, especially in the work-from-home culture:

- Block out time in your calendar to "get stuff done" when work piles up but you have endless meetings.
- Get up and stretch for a couple minutes – at least every hour.
- Rather than taking lunch at your desks, don't be afraid to take a "real" lunch break once in a while. If you can't make a quick run to a local eatery, at least get some lunch and sit down to eat at your dining room table.
- Between calls, crank up a motivational song – something that "gets your motor going." *Alexa, play RISE by Herb Alpert.*
- Give a little affection to the children or pets – or both.
- Go check the mail outside.

And once in a while, don't be afraid to buy that one doughnut for yourself that gives you a trip down memory lane. For me, it's a chocolate éclair.

We can never know about the days to come
But we think about them anyway
And I wonder if I'm really with you now
Or just chasin' after some finer day

Anticipation, anticipation
Is makin' me late
Is keepin' me waitin'

Carly Simon, *Anticipation*, 1971

Looking forward to a little down time in a vacation can make the weeks leading to it just a little brighter.

We work so that we can live (pay bills, eat, have a home, drive a car, etc.). We should never "live to work." While we should always strive to enjoy our jobs, our jobs are not the completeness of our lives – only a part. That's why I like to know something about people that is NOT about what they do for work but rather what makes them different among their peers.

So, when your next planned vacation is approaching, break out the plans (even if it's merely to binge watch the TV). Get ready to enjoy the extra time away. See what it does to the days leading up to your absence.

Every once in a while, you should consider adjusting your focus.

From a literal standpoint, the American Optometric Association encourages us to follow a "20-20-20 rule.[x]"

> *The average American worker spends seven hours a day on the computer either in the office or working from home. To help alleviate digital eyestrain, follow the 20-20-20 rule; take a 20-second break to view something 20 feet away every 20 minutes.*

This is good for the eyes. But what about the heart and mind?

While I cannot give you a hard-and-fast rule, you should change your "mental focus" a few times a day as well. That's why we have regular breaks and a lunch hour. Get up from the desk, walk around the office (or your home), get a drink or some munchies, pet the pooch, or whatever else you need to do to realize there is more to life than just meetings and what's on the screen.

Clearly there are days when the hundreds of e-mails, continual escalations, phones, pings, and everything else tugging at you can't allow the scheduled time. But you need to do what you can to do more than survive.

Adjust your focus.

Smile, you're on candid camera! In this case, it's about being face-to-face with people, not about the nostalgic show.

E-mail and chats while working from home are a reality of the post-Covid world. But what has been lost is the face-to-face contact. Now that many (most?) folks in the Corporate World are going to work from home for the rest of their days, we should still consider picking up the phone (or headset) from time to time to make our point. Here's why:

- There is no inflection, no emphasis, no temperament in an e-mail or a chat.
- There is no ability to convey intent in an e-mail compared to talking on the phone or being face-to-face.
- The probability of a message being completely misunderstood is extremely high.
- In an e-mail, passionate and heartfelt communication can be easily misconstrued as a personal attack.

So, when in doubt, call. Or go to that person and speak directly if you're in the same office. And if you're working from home, it would never hurt to turn the camera on. While I don't have my camera on 100% of the time, I have taken to putting it on more often. Of course, you have to be careful with your mannerisms because everyone can see you rolling your eyes in one of those "here we go again" moments that are bound to happen. But shouldn't we get back to kindness and courtesy?

No one is going to be upset at you if you aren't completely dolled up for a meeting – or at least no one should. And no one will be upset if your kids or dogs occasionally photo-bomb you in the meeting. Again, in the post-Covid world, most everyone understands. And it can break the ice and even make the relationship with clients and colleagues that much stronger. Just be presentable.

Come to think of it, this isn't necessarily about just being face-to-face…it's about building or renewing relationships.

And now for a somewhat sensitive topic: asking for help.

It's one of the hardest things to admit in today's culture of "I can do this" (especially from someone like me who tries to motivate you). But asking for assistance is vital to success in corporate life, success at home, and in some cases life itself. First, let's dispel a myth:

Asking for help is not a sign of weakness.

Go back and read that previous sentence. While we should always strive to do our best and to learn & grow, you can't do it all and you don't know it all.

Now that we have that out of the way, it helps to have a few pointers after you have asked for help:

- Write it down. Keep some form of notes, whether it's an iPad, a sticky note, a memo book or a OneNote. And if the information you need is listed somewhere else, just put a link into the notes.
- Make sure you fully understand before you say, "I got it."
- Before asking a question, check your notes to see if you have already asked and written it down.

When it comes to things beyond mere "knowledge," asking for help may be more difficult. But consider how much time can be saved (using a simple example) if there were two or three people looking for your keys instead of just yourself.

For the life-or-death situations, I must encourage you to seek the professional help needed quickly. Use the benefits package. Whether it's medical- or mental-related, if you need help, you need help. Reach out. I would rather hear you vent for a time than to hear or speak your eulogy.

Finally, if you are the one being asked for help, then you are being trusted beyond what can be explained. Don't brush the request aside. And don't break that trust. Sit down. Put aside the distractions (no multi-tasking). Listen. Help.

Motivation Killers

While I do my best to stay positive in sharing my experience and knowledge, a book like this cannot be completed without the "flip side" of motivation. It can take years, even decades, to get people to a proper and consistent mindset of motivation. But that motivation can be destroyed in seconds. So here are some pitfalls to avoid if you want to keep others looking forward to starting the day.

Note that many of these will fall under the theme of "management," but it goes a long way to crush bad habits early, no matter what your position.

Thursday Motivation

Sun	Mon	Tue	Wed	Thu	Fri	Sat
		1	2	3	4	5

Show up on time. Frankly, this is one of my biggest pet peeves in corporate life. Whether it's a doctor's appointment, church, a meeting, or just whenever you're expected to be somewhere. When it comes to meetings, one of the biggest time wasters in the meeting is having to start over because someone was late and demands that "we" cover what's already been discussed. For my part, I'm usually 5 minutes early so I can exchange pleasantries early and start the meeting on time. One final point about that – if you are consistently late to meetings (I'm going to say it), you are arrogant, rude, and disrespectful of everyone's time. Fix it.

Make rewards … rewarding. All too often, managers tend to reward the diligent with more work. Just because someone **can** excel beyond what they're already doing, you shouldn't make that the only reason to pile the work onto someone's in-box, especially if it doesn't come with any other incentive. Yes, we always have to do more with less. That's reality. But if you don't spread the work out to others who **should** pick up the slack and only give it to those who **will**, you're going to lose your best people.

Let people finish speaking. I don't give a whit about whether you disagree with someone or how important your point is. To continually cut off others in a meeting will shut them down. Naturally, there's a balance. You don't want a meeting hijacked. You don't want a sensitive subject overrunning the purpose of a meeting or call. But it will kill motivation if someone keeps getting cut off before finishing a point.

Don't hijack a meeting. If the purpose of a meeting is plain, and there is limited time, you will do well to take some notes for a private e-mail or create a sidebar meeting for something that is related but only for a few people. How many times have you gone into a meeting with hundreds of people, and it suddenly gets dominated by one or two bellyachers?

Don't play politics. You know the type. The person who talks out of both sides of his or her mouth for so long that the center of his or her lips are sewn shut. Be the same person, whether you're appearing before the Board of Directors or with your team.

Keep your promises. Even the simple things. Be a man or woman of your word. For example, if you say you're going to give a person a particular day off, then let them have it. And on that note, only make promises you can keep.

Allow people to challenge the status quo. Too many motivation-killers will use, "We've always done it that way" without offering any other reason to squash change. And that is the flimsiest excuse one can offer.

Knock off the "breaking down silos" BS. In my more than 30 years working in Corporate America, I've heard it all too often during a reorganization: "We're going to break down the silos." Utter bull! All that happens is that silos are picked up (figuratively) and moved around in a different fashion. I've begun suspecting that too many corporate reorganizations are merely the result of someone trying to prove their college thesis to be worthy of the "A" the professor failed to give.

Fix what's broken. Rather than presenting a shiny new feature, many clients throughout the Corporate World simply want you to admit that your product, software, or service has some flaws and needs maintenance. Don't distract the need for improvement with the latest fad.

Avoid workarounds. In the early-90s, I had a minivan that was leaking oil – badly. I went into the auto parts store to buy a case of oil. The lady behind the counter wanted to know what filter I needed. I said that this was only to keep oil in the engine – that it was leaking. She asked what ended up being painfully obvious after the fact: "why not fix the leak?" Duh! I invested a few dollars in the right gaskets and stopped leaking oil. Money and time saved. In the same way, workarounds may be easier for one person, but a massive waste for others. Fix it once for a thousand clients instead of fixing it a thousand times.

Praise publicly. Want to put a smile on someone's face that is hard to remove? Bring up their accomplishments & victories for all to see. I've said it before, but it bears repeating…there is no such thing as a small victory.

Admonish privately. When it comes to the opposite of praise, correcting a colleague must be done privately. Want to send someone packing, never to return? Correct them in front of others, especially in front of a client or close friend. That's a recipe for immediate reduction. You'll lose good people who may have only needed a quiet word of correction privately to improve. Instead, when you publicly embarrass someone, you've lost them for good – even if they stay with the company.

Other books by Andy Hefty

Dear Mom Don't Worry: A collection of poems between a mother and her USMC recruit

Dear Mom Please Help Me: A collection of poems about troubled troops and veteran suicide

Dear Mom Please Listen: A collection of poems dealing with Autism, Down Syndrome, and other disabilities

Dear Mom Take Heart: Poems about motherhood in all ages and stages

...Always A Marine: Practical advice from a veteran's experience, expertise, and errors

For more information, visit https://dearmomdontworry.com/

Endnotes

Thursday Motivation

Sun	Mon	Tue	Wed	Thu	Fri	Sat
		1	2	3	4	5

i https://www.businessinsider.com/inspirational-quote-of-the-day-2011-11

iiii https://www.imdb.com/title/tt0091187/quotes/?ref_=tt_trv_qu

iii https://pressboxonline.com/2020/09/06/cals-big-night-ripken-berman-remember-2131/

iv https://www.imdb.com/title/tt2488496/quotes/?ref_=tt_trv_qu

v https://www.imdb.com/title/tt5239020/?ref_=ttep_ep12

vi https://www.thoughtsnlife.com

vii https://en.wikipedia.org/wiki/Livin%27_on_a_Prayer

viii https://snoopy.com

ix Taken from a newsletter from Author James Clear

x https://www.aoa.org/healthy-eyes/eye-and-vision-conditions/computer-vision-syndrome

Made in the USA
Columbia, SC
14 June 2024

36613041R00078